For magnanimity, virtue, and love for humanity all together

LIBRARY OF CONGRESS CATALOGING-IN-PUBLICATION DATA
Names: Demi, author. • Title: Confucius : great teacher of China / Demi.
• Description: First edition. | New York : Shen's Books, an imprint of
Lee & Low Books, 2016. | In-house editor, Cheryl Klein. | Audience: Age
8+ | Includes bibliographical references. • Identifiers: LCCN 2015016672 |
ISBN 9781620141939 (hardcover : alkaline paper) • Subjects: LCSH:
Confucius—Juvenile literature. | Philosophers—China—Biography—Juvenile
literature. | Teachers—China—Biography—Juvenile literature. | Politicians—
China—Biography—Juvenile literature. | China—History—To 221 B.C.—
Juvenile literature. • Classification: LCC B128.C8 D46 2016 | DDC 181/.112
[B]—dc23 • LC record available at https://lccn.loc.gov/2015016672

CONFUCIUS
Great Teacher of China

DEMI

SHEN'S BOOKS
an imprint of
LEE & LOW BOOKS INC.
New York

CONFUCIUS
551 BCE–479 BCE

In China, he is known as Kongzi, or "Master Kong." In the West, he is known by the Latinized form of his name: Confucius.

Confucius was a joyous man as well as a great teacher and philosopher. He once said, "I was not born with knowledge, but I am quick to seek it." Though the facts of his life are shrouded in legend, the truths he found have influenced the world for generations.

Many Chinese people feel that no matter the political situation or their religious inclinations, they are followers of Confucius at heart.

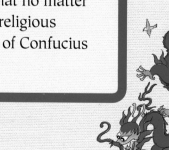

Huang He River

Beijing ◎

YAN

Tianjin ◎

Bohai Sea

JIN

Linzi •

QI

Xiagu •

Yi •

WEI

Qufu •

LU

Yellow Sea

Wei River

QIN

Xi'an ◎

ZHOU

Chengzhou •

ZHENG

CAO

Kuang •

SONG

She •

CAI

CHEN

Huang He River

CHU

Nanjing ◎

◎Wuhan

Yangzi River

WU

Shanghai ◎

Chongqing ◎

YUE

N

CHINESE STATES AT THE TIME OF CONFUCIUS
• **Ancient City**   ◎ Modern City   **STATE**

Tradition says that in the year 551 BCE, a rare and beautiful *qilin* emerged from a forest in the Chinese state of Lu. When it appeared before a young woman praying near Mount Mu, she recognized it as a lucky omen and tied a red ribbon around its horn. The qilin gave her a jade tablet carved with the words, "Your child will be a king without a crown."

Soon after, the young woman gave birth to Confucius.

Some legends say the baby looked very much like his father, a retired soldier with a great bulge on his head. Others say the child was handsome, brilliant, and full of charm. One adds that a comet, two protective dragons, and five old men representing the planets and stars appeared in the sky to celebrate Confucius's birth, and all the birds in the land sang from the trees.

Confucius always believed in the importance of ritual. As a young boy, he loved to dress up in ceremonial robes and act out rites with his friends.

Yet Confucius's early life was also marked by sadness. In 548 BCE, when he was only three years old, his father died. "We were humble and poor when I was young; that's why I can do so many practical things," he said later.

Confucius grew up to be very tall, and exceedingly strong and energetic. He enjoyed hunting, fishing, archery, and working with horses. But of all his activities, he loved reading and studying most, pursuing them with genuine passion. He remarked, "At fifteen, I set my heart on learning."

In 533 BCE, when Confucius was eighteen, he married a young woman named Qiguan. When they had a son, they nicknamed him Liyu, which means "large carp" or "big fish," because on the day of his birth, a neighbor brought a carp, which was an auspicious gift.

Chinese society at that time emphasized that children should obey parents, wives should obey husbands, common people should obey leaders, and everyone should know their places. It was believed this orderly living would bring continual harmony and peace.

As a dutiful son and father, Confucius took many jobs to support his family. He served as a clerk in a granary, and later worked as a keeper of sacred oxen and sheep.

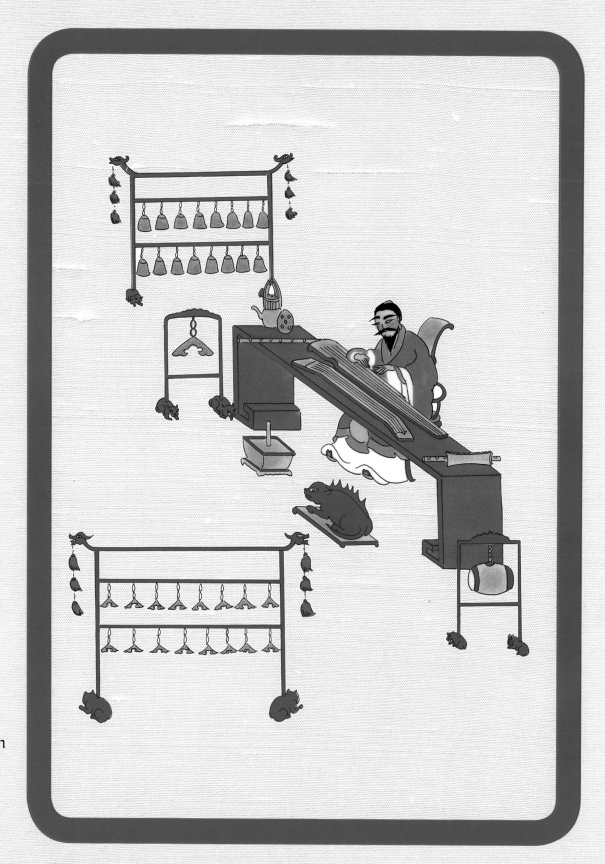

Still, Confucius nurtured his passion for learning, studying history, religion, and music whenever he could.

Tradition says that he once traveled to Chengzhou, the capital city of the Zhou dynasty. There he met Laozi, the great philosopher who established Taoism and served as court librarian to the king. The two men's views were very different: Laozi taught that everyone should lead simple lives devoted to meditation and the study of nature, while Confucius believed in a well-disciplined society where people were involved in public service.

Confucius had developed these views in response to the chaotic world he saw around him. After six centuries of rule, the Zhou dynasty was collapsing into turmoil. The king had no power, and the rich aristocrats continually fought one another, splintering the country into many warring states. The poor were taxed to support the rich, and if the harvests failed, thousands of peasants starved.

All this misery affected Confucius deeply. A society is a living thing, he believed. To bring this suffering to an end, society itself would need to change. It should work for the good of everyone, not just the powerful. But Confucius knew that would require a revolution in the thinking and actions of both the rulers and the people.

As Confucius considered his society, he realized that the most important quality someone could possess was *ren* (仁, pronounced "ren"), compassion or love for other human beings. He also believed in the importance of *de* (德, "duh"), virtue—acting according to moral standards. A person who practiced de acquired *yi* (義, "ee"), righteousness. De and yi could then be demonstrated through *li* (禮, "lee"), correctness in all actions, rituals, speech, and behavior. Li was important because manners and customs were the cement that held a society together.

If an individual developed all these qualities, that person would have wisdom, or *zhi* (知, "jur"). Ren and zhi together would indicate that someone was a *junzi* (君子, "jwun-dze"), a superior human being. Junzi were the people who were most fit to lead others.

"If leaders love ritual, the people cannot be anything but reverent," Confucius said. "If leaders love duty, the people cannot be anything but humble. If leaders love standing by their words, the people cannot be anything but sincere. Once this is done, people from all four corners of the earth will come to the land."

If rulers governed with zhi and ren, their work would be easy and the people would be content. In a tumultuous and violent world, Confucius was the first philosopher to propose compassion as a virtue that leaders should exercise, and as an act that could bind people together into a society.

Confucius looked for a government position where he could put his righteous ideas into practice. But none of the powerful regional rulers wanted to hear that they should be kinder to their people and demonstrate more virtue themselves.

Confucius decided that the best way to influence society was through education, so more people might acquire the skills and knowledge to govern.

In 529 BCE, when he was twenty-two, Confucius became a tutor. He taught many subjects, including poetry, religious and court rituals, music, languages, literature, history, government, writing, and mathematics. He was such an inspiring teacher that his reputation soared.

Eventually, Confucius opened an entire school to spread his ideas. Only the wealthy usually received an education, but Confucius insisted that all young men were welcome to learn, so everyone might have an equal chance to lead. Soon he had many students, rich and poor, who were drawn to his joyous, magnetic personality. "Study as if you'll never know enough," he told them, "as if you're afraid of losing it all."

Confucius taught his pupils the ancient rites and ceremonies that all government officials needed to know, but he also encouraged his students to think for themselves. "If they're not eager to learn, I don't enlighten them," he commented. "If they're not struggling to put it into words, I don't assist them. I hold up one corner to show them, and if they can't come back with the other three, then I don't go on."

Confucius conducted lessons by asking questions of his students, then responding to their answers. "Shall I teach you what knowledge is?" he asked. "When you know a thing, recognize that you know it, and when you do not know a thing, recognize that you do not know it. That is knowledge." He held classes anywhere he liked—hiking in the mountains, strolling down a pathway, or sitting under an apricot tree—and he often told jokes and teased his students. Yet he also emphasized the need for order in both a society and individual thought.

"If you do not understand the will of Heaven, you will have no way to become a junzi. If you do not understand ritual, you will have nowhere to take your stand. If you do not understand words, you will have no way to know people."

While Confucius taught, he continued to look for a government position. Finally, Duke Ding of Lu appointed him governor of a small district called Chungtu.

Confucius did so well as governor that in 501 BCE, he was made the police commissioner of Lu. Legend says that he instantly brought peace and harmony to the entire state. Though doors were left unlocked, there were no burglaries, and lost objects were always returned to their owners.

But Duke Ding was not the ideal moral ruler Confucius hoped to serve. Ding accepted bribes of jewels and horses, and once allowed eighty dancing girls to distract him from his duties. Confucius wanted to find an enlightened ruler who would agree with his ideas about government and right behavior.

So in 497 BCE, Confucius left Ding's court and began traveling with his devoted students, looking for another government post and teaching along the way.

Wandering through the warring states brought Confucius many wild and dangerous adventures. He was often cold and hungry, and more than once, he was nearly killed by bandits or his political enemies.

Confucius journeyed for more than ten years, but in the words of one biographer, he was "too great for the world to accept." His honesty and idealism kept him from fitting in anywhere. Rulers humiliated him many times, and gossips compared him to a dog looking for a bone.

But Confucius never lost his sense of humor, and he was supported by his faithful disciples, who continued to absorb his wisdom.

He taught them that the moral purpose of humanity is to make ourselves better. "If, on examining himself, a man finds nothing to reproach himself for, what worries and fears can he have?" he said.

When asked what he would do if he ran a government, Confucius replied that he would correct language. "If language is incorrect, then what is said does not match what was meant, so what needs to be done cannot be carried out. If what needs to be done cannot be carried out, then rituals and music will not flourish.

"When rituals and music wither, punishments and penalties miss their target. When punishments and penalties miss their target, the people do not know where they stand. Therefore, whatever someone thinks, they must be able to express; and whatever they say, they must be able to do." In matters of language, nothing should be left to chance, he said.

In both government and private life, perhaps the most important word to Confucius was *shu* (恕, "shoo"), which means "compassion" or "open-heartedness." Practicing shu with others would create a peaceful and harmonious world.

Five hundred years before Jesus set forth the Golden Rule, Confucius stated his own Golden Mean: "Never impose on others what you would not choose for yourself."

In 484 BCE, when Confucius was sixty-seven, he returned to his home state of Lu. He had suffered and been humiliated, and he never found the position he sought.

Now he no longer wanted to rule. Confucius was happy spending time with his books, studying and writing. He edited and contributed to many classic Chinese texts, including books of poetry, ritual, and history, and the *Book of Changes*, commonly called the *I Ching*.

Confucius had also succeeded as an educator. His philosophy was alive and thriving. He had taught hundreds of students who could spread his wonderful ideas about human behavior and a compassionate society. Confucian learning and spiritual instruction would form the basic education of the people who governed China for the next 2400 years.

Legend has it that in 479 BCE, a strange animal was killed in the state of Lu. No one knew what it was, so they put it in a wagon and brought it to Confucius.

Confucius realized it was the very same qilin that had come out of the forest to greet his mother before he was born. It still wore shreds of the ribbon she had tied around its horn more than seventy years earlier.

The death of a qilin was a very bad omen, and Confucius believed it foretold his own death.

Shortly thereafter, at the age of seventy-two, Confucius became very ill. All his disciples watched over him.

Confucius said, "The great mountain must crumble, the strong beam bursts, the wise man must wither away like a plant. . . . Find the path to Heaven in the morning, and it won't matter if you die in the evening."

After that he announced, "I wish to speak no more."

Confucius died seven days later.
His faithful students buried him
in the city of Qufu.

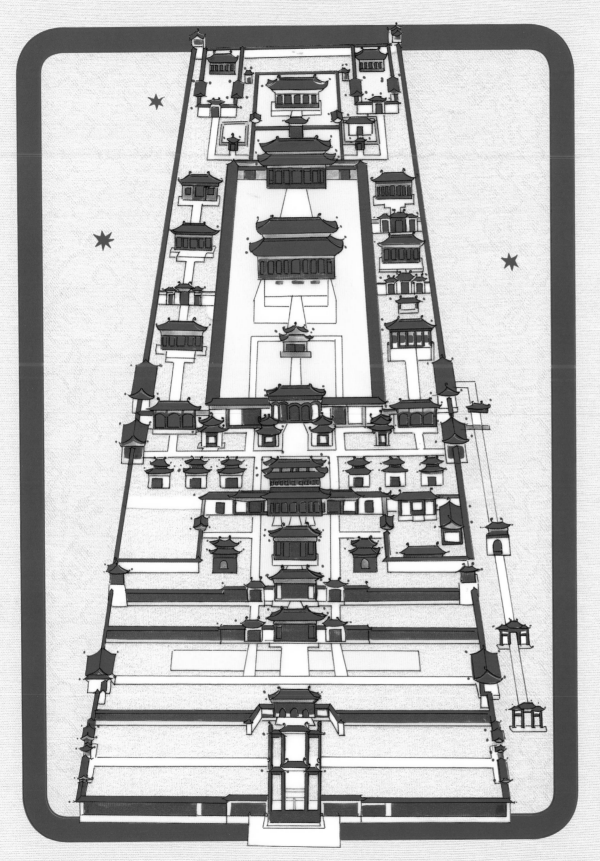

His disciples built a temple on the site, and for more than two thousand years, his grave has been visited by a steady stream of pilgrims.

Confucius's disciples and their followers also compiled their master's sayings in a book called the *Lunyu,* which means "dialogues" or "conversations." This book is known in the West as *The Analects,* and it contains the living words of Confucius.

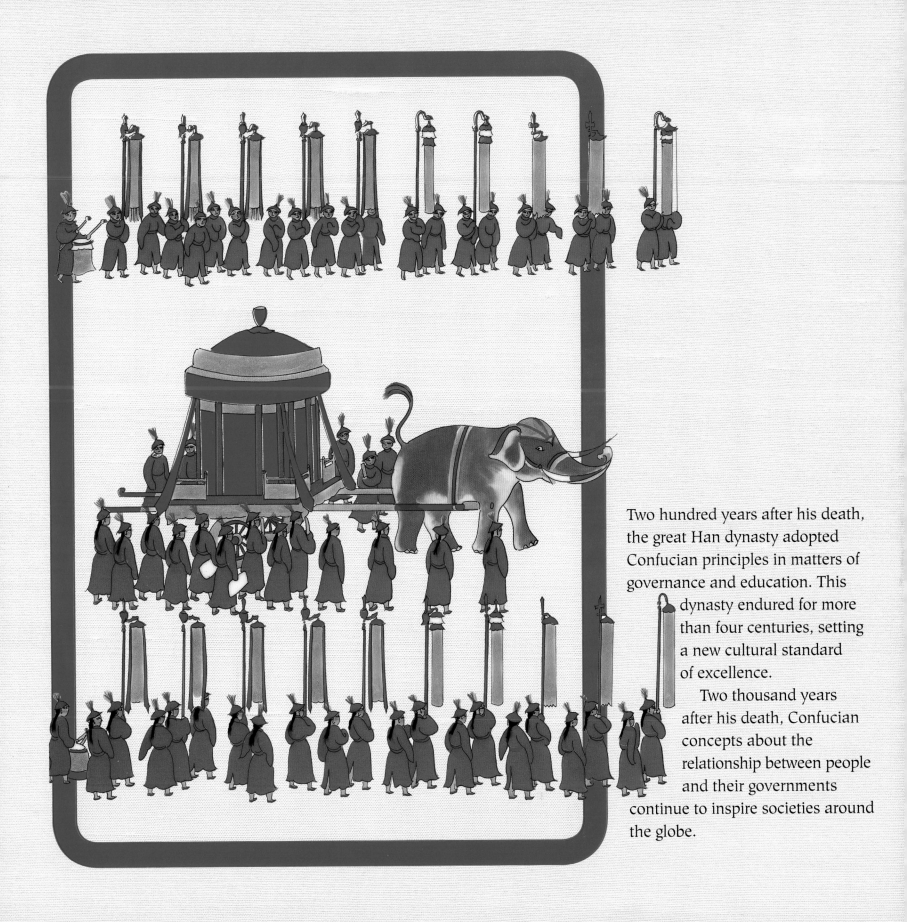

Two hundred years after his death, the great Han dynasty adopted Confucian principles in matters of governance and education. This dynasty endured for more than four centuries, setting a new cultural standard of excellence.

Two thousand years after his death, Confucian concepts about the relationship between people and their governments continue to inspire societies around the globe.

As the qilin foretold, Confucius's influence has been so immense that some still think of him as China's uncrowned king.

SOURCES

Confucius. *Analects*. Translated by David Hinton. Berkeley, CA: Counterpoint, 2014.

——. *The Analects*. Translated by D. C. Lau. New York: Penguin Books, 1979.

——. *The Analects*. Translated by Simon Leys [Pierre Ryckmans], edited by Michael Nylan. New York: W. W. Norton & Co., 2014.

——. *The Analects of Confucius*. Translated by Arthur Waley. New York: Vintage Books, 1989. First published 1938 by Allen & Unwin.

——. *The Analects of Confucius*. Translated by Burton Watson. New York: Columbia University Press, 2007.

McArthur, Meher. *Confucius: A Throneless King*. New York: Pegasus Books, 2011.

Schuman, Michael. *Confucius: And the World He Created*. New York: Basic Books, 2015.

Shaughnessy, Edward L. *Confucian and Taoist Wisdom: Philosophical Insights from Confucius, Mencius, Laozi, Zhuangzi, and Other Masters*. London: Duncan Baird Publishers, 2010.

Szuma Chien. *Selections from "Records of the Historian."* Translated by Yang Hsien-yi and Gladys Yang. South San Francisco: China Books and Periodicals, 1979.

Tsai Chih Chung, ed. and illus., and Goh Beng Choo, trans. *The Sayings of Confucius: The Message of the Benevolent*. Singapore: Asiapac Books, 1989.

Waley, Arthur, ed. and trans. *Three Ways of Thought in Ancient China*. New York: Routledge, 2005. First published 1939 by Allen & Unwin.

Watson, Burton. *Ssu-ma Ch'ien: Grand Historian of China*. New York: Columbia University Press, 1958.

Yu Dan. *Confucius from the Heart: Ancient Wisdom for Today's World*. Translated by Esther Tyldesley. New York: Atria Books, 2009.

QUOTATIONS

Some of the quotations have been lightly adapted for easier reading by a young audience.

Front flap "I was not born": *Analects* 7.20, adapted from the Lau translation.

p. 10 *Analects* 9.6, in the Hinton translation.

p. 11 *Analects* 2.4, in the Lau translation.

p. 19 *Analects* 13.4, adapted from the Hinton translation.

p. 22 "Study as if you'll never know enough": *Analects* 8.17, in the Hinton translation.

p. 22 "If they're not eager to learn": *Analects* 7.8, in the Watson translation.

p. 23 "Shall I teach you what knowledge is?": *Analects* 2.17, in the Waley translation.

p. 23 "If you do not understand the will of Heaven": *Analects* 20.5, adapted from the Watson translation.

p. 27 "Too great for the world to accept": Sima Qian (whose name has also been transliterated as "Szuma Chien" and "Ssu-ma Ch'ien") offers this opinion in his *Records of the Grand Historian*, finished circa 94 BCE.

p. 29 *Analects* 12.4, in the Lau translation.

p. 30 *Analects* 13.3, adapted from the Waley translation.

p. 31 *Analects* 13.3, adapted from the Leys translation.

p. 33 *Analects* 12.2, in the Hinton translation.

p. 39 "The great mountain must crumble": While this does not appear in the *Analects*, Confucius is quoted as saying this in *Selections from "Records of the Historian."*

p. 39 "Learn the path to Heaven": *Analects* 4.8, adapted from the Watson translation.